# ABOUT THIS RESOURCE

A short collection of poems and riddles which aims to assist students in learning some key computing content – both for KS3 content and to prepare for KS4.

I do not recommend trying to commit these to memory per se but instead to use them as a platform to check current learning. Annotating the pages and adding examples etc. will hopefully further deepen understanding.

Online versions with additional content (including more common misconceptions and general computing concepts) can also be found on computingpoetry.weebly.com.

Information has been inspired from free sites online including but not limited to BBC Bitesize, YouTube and exam specification pages.
If you would like to know how I use these with my students, please don't hesitate to contact me – see About Me Page.

*Good luck and happy reading!*

# CONTENTS

# CONTENTS CONT...

# INTRODUCING COMPUTER COMPONENTS - HIPPOS

Hippos is how we remember the components of our PC
It really is that easy- just read on and see!

H is for hardware the things that are physical
I is for input devices, entering things so they're digital
P is for primary memory - R starts our main two
P is for the processor - also known as the CPU
O- is for output so that we can hear and see
S is for secondary storage; our files are not just temporary!

Software of course is needed too; Our programs and apps give us so much to do!

## Questions:
➤ What animal helps us remember the main components?
➤ What do each of the letters stand for?
➤ H is for hardware- the things that are physical. List three pieces of hardware.
➤ Look at line 6 - what is a synonym (another word) for processor.

## Challenge:
➤ For your chosen hardware, can you name whether they're input or output?
➤ 'P is for primary memory - R starts our main two' - What are the main types of primary memory?
➤ Can you make a mind map or other creative project to summarise what you have learnt?

# RIDDLE 1.0

I complete a cycle: fetch, decode, execute

I'm vital for your device to compute

I perform the arithmetic and logic,

To a brain I am analogic

I control operations, which are specified by instructions

1955 is when I got my name,

But calling me a processor means just the same

There are no more clues for you

I'm very clearly the ....

*See next page for answer*

# RIDDLE 1.0 – ANSWER

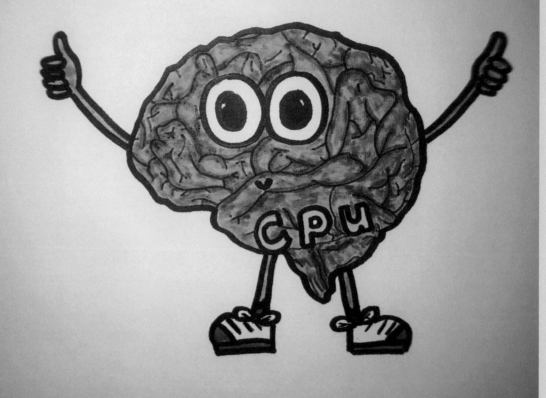

ANSWER - THE CPU

# GENERAL PURPOSE & EMBEDDED SYSTEMS

An embedded system generally has one role,
But a general-purpose computer has no specific goal
The examples are our desktop and laptop
Whereas to list all of embedded – we'd never stop
The components of hippos are what they require
Which includes your fridge, oven and your dryer

It has got a dedicated function in a system that's larger,
And they require less power, so you won't keep needing
your charger
Designing and building is cheaper to do
And typically, the Ram is smaller too!

So to recap: the general-purpose system is the
traditional PC,
Now the differences between them [and embedded]
you can hopefully see!

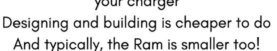

## Questions:
➢ What are the two types of computers?
➢ Can you give an example of each?
➢ How many embedded systems are mentioned?

## Challenge:
➢ In the penultimate (second to last) paragraph
Ram is mentioned. What is Ram?
➢ What does 'dedicated function' mean?
➢ Explain the differences between an embedded
system and a general purpose.

# RIDDLE 2.0

I'm not a device to embed

Guessing me shouldn't lead to a scratch of your head

I've got many uses, not just one

On me lots of things can be done

I can watch videos, do work and surf the net

Sometimes viruses I can also get

A general purpose system I must be,

Not a laptop, so you see


I am of course a ...

*See next page for answer*

# RIDDLE 2.0 – ANSWER

ANSWER - DESKTOP PC

# RIDDLE 3.0

When you're not very hungry you may do me

I'm a number, one more than three

I'm half a byte,

You can get this right

We won't need to quibble

If you tell me I'm a .....

*See next page for answer*

# RIDDLE 3.0 – ANSWER

ANSWER – NIBBLE

# KANGAROO MEASUREMENTS

Happy kangaroos make goo
And bad kangaroos do too

Why do we remember this phrase?
Well, it's one of our quirky ways
For our order of measures to be recalled
So we won't have a grade that leaves us appalled!

For Hertz we remember our happy kangaroos
For bytes it's the bad ones making goo too
That gives us the order: kilo, mega, giga
Plus terra if we need our storage even bigger!

This of course goes from small to big,
Remembering them really isn't a hard gig.
For conversions you won't really need to learn much more
Other than to go up each one, multiply by one thousand and twenty four (1024)

## Questions:
➢ What is the saying to help us remember the order of measurements?
➢ List the measurements from smallest to largest.
➢ Look at the last line: our conversion between the units is 1000 bits or ...?

## Challenge:
➢ How many bytes are in two MB?
➢ A nibble is four bits, can you find out what we call two nibbles?
➢ What does bit stand for?

# MALWARE

Malware means malicious software,
Causing harm to our devices whilst we're blissfully unaware
A virus causes disruption and often damage too
It also replicates and tries to find another device to pass through

A human must do something for the virus to open and infect
downloading email attachments and software could easily cause a
defect
A worm whilst similar does not need human action to spread
Just connecting to a device that has a worm is enough for it to move
ahead

A Trojan is perhaps the most sly
Pretending to be a gift (just like the trojan horse myth) or acts an ally
You won't expect the damage to be done,
Because it disguises itself as something good or fun.

Spyware does harm the device in the same way,
It puts you at risk when you work or play
e.g. keyloggers and browser hijackers will record your personal data
and pass them on to the spyware creator

Ransomware is the last malware for us to go through
It's basically hackers blackmailing you
They block access or make files so that it cannot be read
They really can cause a lot of dread

WannaCry is a famous example which targeted the NHS
This caused worldwide damage, a loss of millions/billons, and a
whole lot of stress!

*Continued on next page...*

# MALWARE CONT....

## Questions:
➤ What does malware mean?
➤ Provide some examples of malware.
➤ A virus replicates. What does replicate mean?
➤ Malware can slow your computer down. What other effects can they have?

## Challenge:
➤ Define a hacker. Can you name the types?
➤ Why does the trojan have its name?
➤ What is WannaCry an example of? Can you find another example?

# SIGNS OF A PHISHING EMAIL

There are certain signs of phishing emails for which you should be aware
When sending out communication professional companies will take a lot of care

So SPAG : spelling, punctuation and grammar should be correct,
And non-personalised greetings are also a little suspect

Also check for the sender's name
And that the link and the destined address are the same

A sense of urgency should also raise distrust
If you feel doubt, ringing the company is an absolute must!

Phishers try get recipients to click on the link to enter their personal details
but knowing these signs will help cause their attempts of theft to fail

## Questions:
➢ SPAG must be correct. What does SPAG stand for?
➢ What are the signs of a phishing email?
➢ What do you think you should do if you receive a phishing email?

## Challenge:
➢ Phishers pretend to be from a legitimate company. What does this mean? Provide an example.
➢ Why might a sense of urgency cause mistrust?
➢ Can you find any real-life examples of phishing attacks?

# E-SAFETY

When we're online we need to be kind
There won't be a chance for us to rewind
When we post it's there forever,
So please make sure that you are clever

Do not post anything you won't want others to see
Everyone's a witness: friends, strangers and family
Think of social media as a personal stage
The things you do matter, no matter your age!

Look at Jesy Nelson and the odd one out
Who explores what trolling is all about
Social media can have a huge cost
So many lives are needlessly lost

For words can hurt and go a long way
So be very careful with what you choose to say
Your actions and words can be evidence in years ahead
You don't want to hit any barriers because of what you once said

Paris Brown learnt an unfortunate lesson as a teen
With what can happen when all your tweets can be seen
Her story caused quite a stir
With many having lots to say about her

So really consider what you post - particularly when you're bored
Because you don't want to be trolled or a victim of fraud
Think about what you view and do
And remember you never really know who you're talking to

Your personal details are not something you should share
You really must take a lot of care
The internet can be great and really beneficial to use
But also very risky and dangerous if abused.

*Continued on next page...*

# E-SAFETY CONT....

## Questions:

➢ What is E-Safety?

➢ When we delete a picture from online, it'll remove from devices forever. True or False? Can you explain why?

➢ What are some examples of social media?

➢ What does trolling mean?

## Challenge:

➢ You could be a victim of fraud. Describe fraud.

➢ Jesy Nelson? Paris Brown? Why are they relevant here?

➢ The internet does more harm than good. Evaluate this view.

➢ What tips would you give someone to be safe online?

# RIDDLE 4.0

I am nasty, I am mean
I am relentless, I am keen
I cause upset, I do harass
And my comments can be quite crass

I will pop up on your videos and posts
From me you will hear from the most
You should report me to make me stop
Some say I live under a bridge not on top

But I live online and I commit a crime
When I act it's important someone is told, for I can
take my toll; after all I am an internet...

*See next page for answer*

# RIDDLE 4.0 – ANSWER

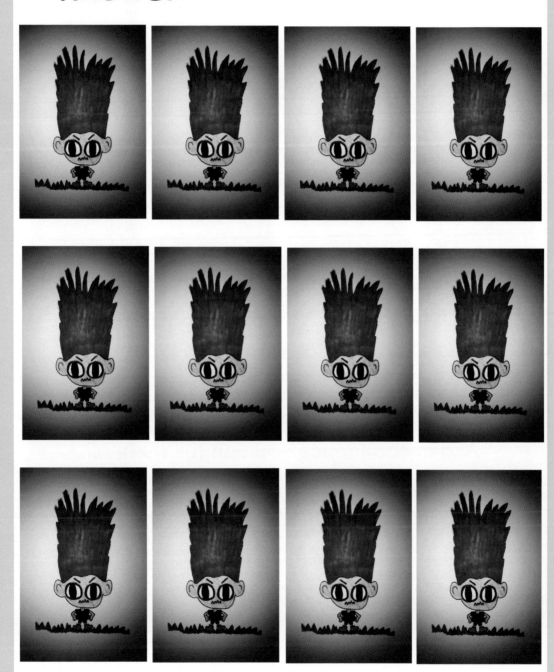

ANSWER - TROLL

# RIDDLE 5.0

Remember you should always talk to someone about
how you feel
As others can help you with how to cope and deal
Sometimes you might just need to be listened to
Especially on days when you're feeling blue

Or you might find yourself at a time
Where you need to report a crime
So this is somewhere where you can go
Especially if you don't want others to know

You can give these people a call
And in confidence you can tell them all
In emergencies you should still call 999
But if you just need support and someone to listen,
you could call...

*See next page for answer*

# RIDDLE 5.0 – ANSWER

ANSWER - CHILDLINE

# COMPUTATIONAL THINKING

Abstraction: removing the irrelevant information, keep just what you need

Decomposition: breaking down the problem so that it's easy to read

Algorithmic thinking: instructions followed one at a time

I hope these computing concepts are now easier with this rhyme!

**Questions:**
➤ How many computational thinking terms have been mentioned?
➤ What does decomposition mean?
➤ What does irrelevant information mean? Can you provide an example where information may be irrelevant?

# ALGORITHMS

What's an algorithm, I hear you ask?
Well, they're ordered instructions to complete a task!

In order they really must be,
Just like you're following a recipe

Flowcharts and pseudocode, we can write
To plan our program and ensure it's right

Symbols have a specific role though,
Is this something that you know?

If not, read flowcharts before you go.

# FLOWCHARTS

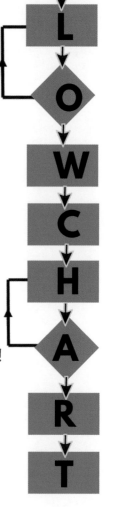

Ovals will show our start and stop
Not always at the bottom but always on top
For repetition we might not need an end
We'll instead use arrows going around a bend

We'll always use arrows – never a line
Unless we want to hear me whine and whine
Arrows are needed to represent data flow,
A yes or no question? in a diamond that must go!

A diamond for a decision- focus on the D
It really does make it very easy!
A parallelogram is for data, going in or out
And a rectangle is what the process is all about

Showing us the steps of what to do…
Now that's all our flowchart shapes gone through!

## Questions:
➤ What shape begins and ends our flowchart?
➤ We always use arrows, we never use…?
➤ What shape is used for decisions? How can we easily remember that?
➤ For input and output we use a ….?

## Challenge:
➤ Flowcharts always need to stop. True or False? Explain your answer.
➤ What data type is a yes or no question?
➤ Provide an example of a process.
➤ Draw the flowchart shapes.

# RIDDLE 6.0

I store what you're on
But lose power then I'm gone
Storing the running OS I also do
And I'm accessed directly by the CPU
I'm easy to access and edit
Have you now got it?

Of course I am:

the ...?

*See next page for answer*

# RIDDLE 6.0 - ANSWER

**Challenge:**

What does RAM stand for?

What else do you know about RAM?

What other memory do you know?

Is RAM hardware or software? Explain why.

ANSWER - RAM

# MEMORY

Directly accessed by the CPU
That's our primary memory- remember the main two
First there's ram, temporarily storing what we're on
But forget to click save and then it's gone!

Being volatile means to save it needs electricity,
It also allows you to access and edit easily!
Next, we have Rom- this enables our computer to start
But to access and edit, we need to be very, very smart!

Is it volatile? No it's not!
Its contents will not be forgot!
There are other examples of memory - e.g. cache and virtual
So keep reading on to become even more intellectual!

## Questions:
➢ What is the definition of primary memory?
➢ What organ is the CPU like? What else do you know about CPU?
➢ Why do we need ROM?
➢ Which memory is volatile? What does this mean?

## Challenge:
➢ Explain two differences between Rom and Ram
➢ State two other examples of primary memory
➢ Find information about cache and virtual memory.

# LEGISLATION

There's different legislation of which you need to be sure,
By legislation I mean following the law
Data Protection Act sets 8 principles to obey,
You must keep data safe every single day

Computer Misuse Act outlines acceptable use,
It is never acceptable to use technology for abuse
Spreading malware or hacking is not right,
Unless of course your hat colour is white

These can legally check the system's secure
As that is what they're getting hired for!
Copyright designs and patents is our last to know,
Copying data without permission is an absolute no

Creative Commons can give some freedom to use and
distribute
But the original author, to them you must attribute
For they have worked hard and it is still their own
So it's important that their name is clearly shown

Breaking these laws could lead to fines and/or jail
So do ensure that you never fail
Follow these laws and keep yourself protected,
You won't like the consequences if illegal activity's
detected!

Continued on next page...

# LEGISLATION CONT...

## Questions:
- What does legislation mean? What legislation is mentioned?
- What happens if you are not in compliance with the legislation?

## Challenge:
- How many principles does the Data Protection Act have?
- What are these principles?
- Explain how you could break each of the legislation.
- Is hacking always illegal? Explain your answer.

# THE DATA PROTECTION ACT

Fairly and lawfully our data must be processed
Accuracy is important- else you'll become stressed
Rights to the data subjects, you must comply
Transferring out the EEA*? don't even try!

Length that data is kept is for as long as it's needed
Adequate data only, this simply cannot be exceeded
Specifically storing for a set purpose is a must
Safe and secure, that is what the data subject trusts

Breaking these 8 principles will result in a fine to pay,
And your company's reputation will start to decay
Security threats and measures- you must be aware,
If you're unsure [re]read the poem on malware.**


*European Economic Area
**available on computingpoetry.weebly.com or pages 14-15

## Questions:
➤ What does EEA stand for?
➤ The person we hold data about is known as the data ...? (look at line 2)
➤ How can we keep data secure?

## Challenge:
➤ 'Your company reputation will start to decay'. Explain why a company cares about their reputation.
➤ Provide a scenario of a company following and breaking the data protection act.

# RIDDLE 7.0

Hardware- I can be an input or output device
I can be cheap, or I can be a very high price!
What's important is that you can touch and see
Even if I'm external or inside your PC
But I am not hardware I am the opposite in fact,
I am something that can be hacked.
I can be bad, I can be good
And I can be something that's misunderstood.
You cannot touch me,
And I can be paid for or I can be free
But if there is no cost to pay
Be careful with what I say
Because sometimes I may tell a lie
Perhaps even acting like a spy
Application and utility are one way to sort
Splitting into proprietary and open source should also be taught
I'm digital, a program and app; sometimes I crash or have a mishap
Sometimes you own my license key & other times you can distribute me!
But regardless of whether you can or can't share
I hope by now you know, that I am describing...

*See next page for answer*

# RIDDLE 7.0 – ANSWER

ANSWER – SOFTWARE

# SOFTWARE

There are different rules for different type of software,
Dictating whether you can [legally]modify or share
The two you need to know for your course*
Is proprietary software and open source

With proprietary software there'll be a license fee
And you'll get good support from a company
Whereas you can use open source without a price
But community support will have to suffice

You can also modify the source code if you desired
But for proprietary explicit permission is required
Changes are absolutely not permitted
Unless you want to risk being committed

So with open source there's much more control for individual
use
Which is great unless your intention is to abuse
Examples are python, Twitter and BBC
Remember for proprietary you need to buy the license key

So Microsoft packages are ones you're likely familiar with
You can use, but there's nothing you can take or give
The software remains just as it's supplied
It belongs to the creator - it is their pride!

Any author or creator should be referenced to,
As it's because of them you can do what you want to do.

Continued on next page...

# SOFTWARE CONT...

## Questions:

➢ Define Software.
➢ What are the two types of software?
➢ What are some examples of Microsoft packages?

## Challenge:

➢ Explain the difference between proprietary and open source software.
➢ If you don't acknowledge the author, which law may you be breaking?

# RIDDLE 8.0

I have the name of a disease
But none of my symptoms are to sneeze
A headache and feeling weak
Swollen glands, which may be obvious in your cheek


A fever of up to 103 degrees Fahrenheit
And I'll cause you to lose your appetite
The operating system is what I help with
If you remember me, five functions I can help give


Do you know? Or are you feeling stumped?
The way to remember these all, is to recall...


## Challenge:

Can you find out some examples of operating systems?
What operating system do you use?


See next page for answer

# RIDDLE 8.0 - ANSWER

ANSWER - MUMPS

# MUMPS-OS

An operating system
has many roles,
You might need to know
these to meet your goals,
So use Mumps
to help you recall,
Five of its main functions-
but no it's not them all!

M is for the management
    of your computer's memory
U is providing a user
    interface- e.g. a GUI
M is for multitasking-
    you can do more than one thing
P- is for peripheral management-
    controlling what goes out and in
S is for system security,
    your username, passwords and files

Now I hope that this helps you get a grade that'll result in all smiles!

## Questions:
➢ Mumps helps us remember key functions of the operating system. What does Mumps stand for?
➢ What memory do we know?
➢ What do we mean by multitasking? Can you provide some examples of multitasking on the computer?

## Challenge:
➢ What does peripheral mean? Can you provide examples?
➢ GUI is a user interface. This stands for graphical user interface. Can you find out about any others?

# USER INTERFACES

The first we shall start with is the Graphical user interface* Now
this can take up quite a bit of space!
However it makes communication quite simple and quick
Including windows icons menus and pointers** to click

Natural language is another choice
You can control this with just your voice
But it may need training to be effective
Else you could get results that are defective

Menu driven gives you options to pick
You're limited in your input but it should be quick
You could have a full screen menu taking up the whole screen
Or a menu bar where options at the top can be seen

These are easy to use ; no commands are needed to be known
You can guess until you find what you want to be shown
However menus can be slow to navigate around
Unlike CLI where results can be immediately found
Popular on ATMs and self-service checkouts
Though perhaps not for those whose jobs are now without

And lastly we have command line interface
Amongst early computers this was commonplace
Users type in commands so that they can interact
A prompt is displayed to enter a command for the pc to enact
Commands need to be correct for it to work as desired
And a level of expertise is therefore required
For these experts, interaction can be of high speed
And many programs can simultaneously proceed
It does not need the memory and processing power of the latest
tech
Command driven programs can often run on machines with a
lower spec

Continued on next page...

# USER INTERFACES CONT...

The amount of commands to learn is its main flaw
All the other interfaces are much easier for sure

When designing a new interface you should try
To have it attractive and pleasing to the eye
Allow for different options to be tested with ease
Use suitable colour groupings with correspondent keys
It should be easy to use with little need for training
Words should be simple without needing explaining
Everyone should be able to use it; there should be no divide
And help documentation would be good to provide
Everybody's needs should really be thought about
Then your interface will be near perfect, of that I have no doubt.

\* GUI pronounced as Goo-ee
\*\* This may be referred to as WIMP

## Questions:

➤ What are the different types of user interfaces?
➤ What does WIMP stand for?
➤ Which user interface is easy to use? Which is difficult to use?
➤ We use menu-driven interface with ATMS. Where else do we use them?
➤ Can you provide examples of natural language interface?

## Challenge:

➤ Why do we need a user interface?
➤ Choose two user interfaces. Describe how they compare.
➤ What are some of the disadvantages of each of the user interfaces?

# COMPRESSION

Compression is the method to reduce the size of a file
So that streaming and sending emails won't take a long while

It also reduces the space on your device
Without requiring a hefty price

The number of bits to store the information is reduced
Lossy gets rid of bits that weren't necessary to be used

It makes similar pixels in images the same
But you'll hardly notice the difference in the frame

Unless you want an image of really high resolution
But if that's the case compression wouldn't be a solution

Once a file's reduced using lossy compression,
Recovering the original quality becomes out of the question

However, with lossless compression this isn't the case
You're not losing this possibility in your saving of space

Lossless compression groups similar data to save room,
But from the original you can later resume

It makes everything compact until you need it once more,
And then the original file you can restore

Generally this method is good with text,
If you used lossy you'd miss the rest

As it would not make much sense without all the detail
Just Imagine trying to read with gaps in your email!

Continued on next page...

# COMPRESSION CONT...

Zip files are a great example to show that you understand
Lossless compression stores files that had long ago been
planned

They can archive work that might be needed later
But they're not so good for storing any current data

Or you might use lossless so you can send /post on the net
Without having lack of storage as a potential threat

Generally lossless compression won't make a file as small
And that's because you get to keep it all

The quality of data will not be altered
And yet your processing speed will not have faltered

Lossless is great for text; lossy for images and sound
But neither should have a loss of quality that is profound!

Compression is also a type of utility software
Now do the next riddle to test your knowledge, if you dare

## Questions:
➢ What is compression (look at line 1)
➢ What are the benefits of compression?
➢ What are any disadvantages?
➢ I have a text file... which compression technique will be used?
Explain why.

## Challenge:
➢ Name the file extensions of different files that are compressed –
e.g. music files can be mp3.
➢ What do I mean by a utility software? Can you find any other
examples?
➢ What is an application software? What are the differences between
utility and application?

# RIDDLE 9.0

Too much memory can make your computer run slow

So some bits may need to go

There are two ways that this can happen

And they're both forms of compression

A utility software which you should also know

And I'm the method used for sound, music and video

I'm used so you that you can store a lot of files

And so that sending data doesn't take a long while


So now take your guess, I'm clearly _____ not lossless!

*See next page for answer*

# RIDDLE 9.0 – ANSWER

ANSWER - LOSSY

# RIDDLE 10.0

I'm not an input device, I am out

I'm not affected if you decide to shout

So speakers and headphones, I am not

I'm popular for all ages, from adults to tots


Sometimes with a touch, I can interact

But other times, I won't even react

I am hardware so I must be physical

A display is also what I may be called


Another word for me is also a screen

And on me things can be seen

I can be related to a PC or TV

I'm called a _____ though, yes that is me!


*See next page for answer*

# RIDDLE 10.0 – ANSWER

ANSWER - MONITOR

# GLOSSARY FOR USES ONLINE

**E-safety** – making sure when you're online you take care

**Personal details** – information you don't want to share

**Chat room** –   virtual rooms where you talk to people you don't know
please don't use these, the dangers can be found below!
grooming, abuse, bribing to name just a few
talking to strangers is something you should not do!

**Catfishing** – when you're online and pretending to be someone you're not

**Viral videos** – enough views that everyone thinks 'wow that's a lot'

**Cyber bully** – bullying someone online using technology

**Troll** – leaving nasty comments without apology

**Click bait** – offering enticement to tempt you to click

**Ghosting** – ignoring someone until they've picked up on your trick
once they've clued up to the act
they'll stop making contact
of course it's kinder to explain and say bye
instead of leaving people thinking why

**Creeping** – where you follow someone so closely–it's like you obsess

**Filtering** – limiting and restricting what you can access

**Block** – stopping someone from seeing what you do

**Report** – report concerns to protect others too

**CEOP** –   a place for online protection and advice
just like teachers, parents and friends; people to confide in when
others aren't being nice

**Https** – means the site you're on is secure

**Http** – is your data safe? Well you can't be sure...

*Continued on next page...*

# GLOSSARY FOR USES ONLINE CONT....

Please be aware of the dangers online and keep yourself
protected
Be wary too of your computer becoming infected

If data becomes corrupt or your device runs slower
You could have malware or an unwanted follower
Hackers get in to your device when they have no right
Well unless their hat colour is white

And malware is bad software meant to harm
If you suspect you have this: remain calm!
Read the poems to find out what to do
Or take it to a professional- they'll help make your device like
new

Technology can be really helpful in what you do-
But there's lots of dangers present too
Yes I know technology can really be great!
But please be aware of the risks- before it's too late!

## Questions:
➤ What is a catfish? Why might someone catfish?
➤ We should block and report trolls and cyberbullies. Why?
➤ Explain what is meant by a viral video. Can you think of any
examples?
➤ Who can we report E-Safety concerns to?

## Challenge:
➤ What's the difference between HTTP and HTTPS?
➤ The legal hacker has what colour hat? What do we call illegal
hackers? What is the difference between them?
➤ Create a creative project: flashcards, mindmap etc. on the key
words.

# A NOTE OF THANKS....

Thank you for taking the time to give this a read,

I hope they've given you some information that you need

Or at least provided you with a good start

Especially if you've learnt them off by heart!

I do hope that they have helped with your computing knowledge - I really do

And I wish lots and lots of success to come to you!

# INSPIRED WORK

Use this space if you would like to add some illustrations / diagrams with for what you have learnt. Perhaps you want to write your answers here or even give your own riddles/poems a go?

# INSPIRED WORK

Use this space if you would like to add some illustrations / diagrams with for what you have learnt. Perhaps you want to write your answers here or even give your own riddles/poems a go?

# ABOUT ME

With only teaching KS3 at the moment (I am at a start-up school, but I tutor KS4), I am using the opportunity to explore creative projects such as these! I hope students find the poems and riddles enjoyable and hopefully a good way to understand and learn computing content.

This booklet provides a fun and unique method of delivering content from the National Curriculum for Computing in England, as well as equipping students with knowledge on how to be a responsible digital citizen. This can be used as a stand alone resource or in conjunction with other booklets in this series.

Questions and challenges are included throughout to further develop understanding. The answers for these can be found easily through independent research or by downloading the accompanying answer booklet free of charge (found on www.computingpoetry.weebly.com and TES).

If you would like any more information or would like to provide any feedback (I'd appreciate to hear your thoughts!) then please reach out via my website/email/twitter:

*Computingpoetry.weebly.com*
*Email: toughcomputing@gmail.com*
*Twitter: @tough_Miss*

Printed in Great Britain
by Amazon

75481345R00029